AFTER THE EARTHQUAKE

BY WILLIAM McCAY

Table of Contents

Earthquake!

Have you ever been on a plane during a storm? You shake and bounce around, and you wish you were back on solid ground. Think how scary it is when you are on solid ground, and the ground begins to shake! That's what happens during an **earthquake**.

During a small earthquake, you will feel a little shaking. Pictures hanging on the walls might move back and forth. Dishes might rattle inside the kitchen cabinet. A lamp might possibly fall and break. In all likelihood no one will be hurt.

In a very strong earthquake, you might be thrown upward or down to the ground. Cracks might appear in the ground. Windows might shatter. Buildings and bridges might collapse. People might be injured or even killed.

A strong earthquake caused the crack in this highway. The white lines show how far the ground shifted.

A parking garage collapses after an earthquake in California in 1994.

Strong earthquakes often snap electrical wires. That means electric lights and machines will not work. Water pipes sometimes break, so people have no water to drink. Pipes that carry natural gas, and tanks that hold gasoline and dangerous chemicals, can break and start fires.

A parking garage collapses after an earthquake in California in 1994.

Firefighters try to put out a fire in a collapsed building after an earthquake in Taiwan on September 21, 1999.

3

What causes the shaking during an earthquake? The surface of our planet is made of pieces of rock that fit together like the pieces of a jigsaw puzzle. The pieces of rock are called **tectonic (tek-TAHN-ik) plates**. When these plates move, the ground shakes.

This map shows the tectonic plates that form Earth's surface. Earthquakes are caused by shifting plates.

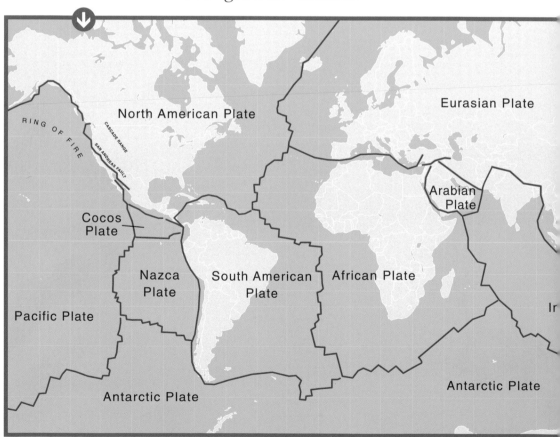

RING OF FIRE

CASCADE RANGE

SAN ANDREAS FAULT

North American Plate

Eurasian Plate

Arabian Plate

Cocos Plate

Nazca Plate

South American Plate

African Plate

Pacific Plate

Ir

Antarctic Plate

Antarctic Plate

This photo shows where two plates meet on the west coast of the United States. It is called the San Andreas Fault.

RING OF FIRE

Pacific Plate

stralian Plate

seismogram

Aftershocks are mini-quakes that come after the main part of an earthquake is over. They can cause even more damage. Aftershocks are especially dangerous for rescue workers who have gone into wrecked buildings to help people who are trapped inside. The buildings can collapse, trapping the rescue workers along with the people they are trying to help.

An earthquake is measured by a **seismometer**, which records **vibrations** in the ground. The seismometer produces a visual record called a **seismogram**.

One scale used to measure the magnitude, or strength, of an earthquake is called the Richter scale.

HOW STRONG IS AN EARTHQUAKE?

RICHTER SCALE

2.5	Generally not felt
3.5	Felt by many people
4.5	Some local damage possible
6.0	A destructive earthquake
7.0	A major earthquake
8.0 AND UP	A great earthquake

Very strong earthquakes can cause **tsunamis (soo-NAHM-eez),** or tidal waves, on the ocean. These monster waves are gigantic ripples caused by earthquake shocks underwater. As these ripples reach the shore, they turn into giant waves as high as sixty feet.

This row of parking meters was bent almost to the street by the force of a tsunami that struck Hawaii in 1963. The tsunami was caused by an earthquake that took place in Chile.

It's a FACT!

During the great Alaska earthquake of 1964, a big fishing boat was caught by a tsunami. The tsunami lifted the boat and set it down in a schoolyard two whole blocks from the ocean shore!

7

This aerial photo shows the results of a landslide in El Salvador on January 18, 2001.

Earthquakes can cause **landslides**. In a landslide, dirt and rocks slide down the sides of a mountain. A landslide can damage buildings and hurt people.

Earthquakes can also cause **avalanches**. In an avalanche, ice and heavy snow slide down a mountainside. An avalanche can be just as dangerous as a landslide.

Snow and ice crash down the side of this mountain during an avalanche.

9

To the Rescue!

Most earthquakes are over in fifteen seconds. As soon as an earthquake is over, people spring into action. Police officers and firefighters go out to rescue people who are hurt or trapped. Hospital workers help people who have been injured.

The army, navy, marines, and the National Guard also help with rescue work. They send people to fight fires, drive ambulances, and bring medical supplies. Specially trained helicopter teams carry people and supplies to help earthquake victims. They also bring injured people to hospitals.

A U.S. Marine gives a lollipop to a Turkish girl who has survived an earthquake.

Groups like the Red Cross send people who are specially trained for rescue work. The Red Cross also provides tents, blankets, food, water, and medicine.

During the India earthquake of 2001, the Red Cross brought 5,000 blankets to wrecked towns.

Often, it is very hard for rescue workers to get to the places that need the most help. Earthquakes often destroy roads, bridges, and airports. Cars and trucks carrying rescue workers and supplies can't get through. Planes must land many miles away. Sometimes rescue workers reach a disaster area by helicopter.

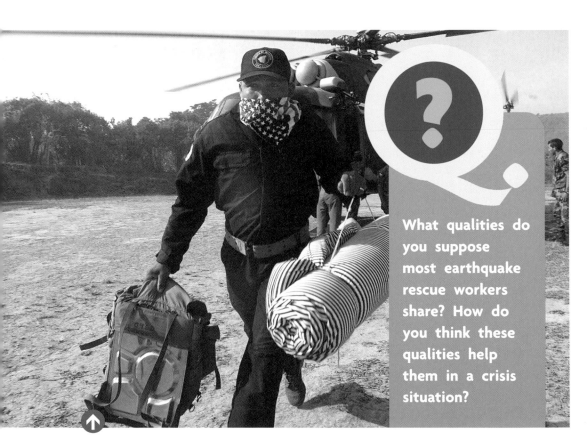

?

What qualities do you suppose most earthquake rescue workers share? How do you think these qualities help them in a crisis situation?

A small town only seventeen miles from El Salvador's capital was cut off during an earthquake in 2001. Rescue workers used helicopters to bring supplies to people.

THE INDIA EARTHQUAKE OF 2001

On January 26, 2001, a 7.9 magnitude earthquake rocked western India. After the quake, people from all over the world came to help. The International Red Cross sent tons of food and medical supplies. Doctors came from Norway and Finland. A French group called Doctors Without Borders also sent a medical team. Denmark sent a whole portable hospital. Rescue teams came from Britain, Germany, and Switzerland. The United States sent a jumbo jet with equipment to purify, or clean, drinking water. Even Pakistan, a country that has fought wars with India, sent tents and blankets for people whose homes had been destroyed.

Western India was the site of the 2001 earthquake.

A Swiss rescue team helps Indian army personnel search for survivors.

This front-page story about the earthquake appeared on January 29, 2001, in an Indian newspaper.

Afterward

This specially trained dog is searching for trapped people.

For the first four days after an earthquake, searchers try to find and rescue trapped people. Sometimes they use dogs to help in the search. Dogs can smell people trapped in the **rubble**.

It's a FACT!

Four days after the earthquake in India in 2001, rescuers dug out a mother and baby. They had been buried when their apartment building collapsed, but they came through without being badly hurt.

After rescue workers have finished their jobs, bulldozers and cranes can go to work clearing the rubble.

A man walks through a street surrounded by earthquake-damaged homes in India in April 2001.

A construction crew cleans up the rubble on a highway after an earthquake in Los Angeles in 1994.

People who have lost their homes may have to live in tents temporarily. Telephones may not work. Often

This tent city was set up for thousands of earthquake survivors in Turkey in 1999.

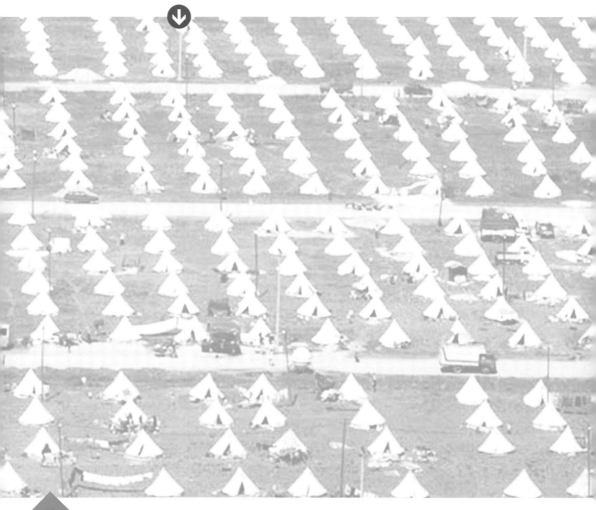

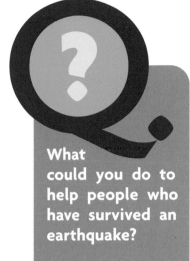

there is no gas, electricity, or plumbing. Drinking water must be cleaned, or else people will get sick. Disease can be one of the worst problems after an earthquake.

What could you do to help people who have survived an earthquake?

Ready to Rebuild

Most cities that have been damaged by earthquakes are rebuilt. People usually choose to rebuild in the same location even though they know another earthquake might occur. Why do they take the risk?

Some of the reasons are personal. People want to stay where they work, play, go to school, and have family and friends. Other reasons are economic. Cities can be important centers for transportation, business, and tourism.

TIMELINE OF MAJOR EARTHQUAKES THAT AFFECTED SAN FRANCISCO

In the last two hundred years, hundreds of earthquakes have affected the San Francisco area. Most were just small tremors that caused no damage. Here are some of the biggest earthquakes in the region that were felt in San Francisco.

Area Affected	San Francisco	Hayward Valley	San Francisco Peninsula	San Francisco Peninsula	East of San Francisco Bay	Hayward Fault	Gilroy	Morgan Hill
Magnitude	6.0	6.75	7.0	5.5	5.75	7.0	6.25	5.75
Year	1808	1836	1838	1856	1864	1868	1897	1899

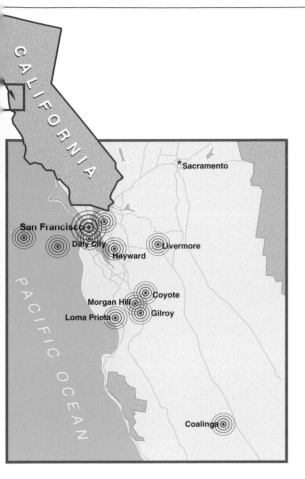

San Francisco is one city that has been rebuilt many times following earthquake damage. It is an important center for business and tourism. It is an important port, and it is also a thriving cultural center.

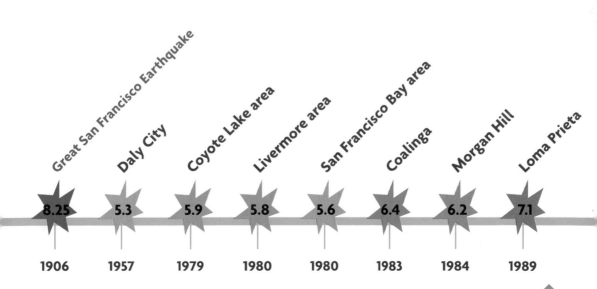

Sometimes cities that have been damaged by earth-quakes cannot be rebuilt in the same location. It is simply too dangerous. People do not want to live there anymore. An example of this is the town of Valdez (val-DEEZ) on the coast of Alaska. During an earth-quake in 1964, part of the town was sucked into the ocean. Valdez was built up again, but not in the same place. The new Valdez is in a safer area nearby.

THE GREAT SAN FRANCISCO EARTHQUAKE AND FIRE OF 1906

On April 18, 1906, at 5:13 a.m., San Francisco was rocked by an enormous earthquake. Some of the city's 410,000 residents were thrown out of bed by the force of the shock. People rushed for doorways or headed to open streets in case their buildings collapsed. Fires were already breaking out.

The quake, estimated to have been 8.25 on the Richter scale, still ranks as the most devasta-ting natural disaster in U.S. his-tory. It was followed by major aftershocks that caused many damaged buildings to collapse. The city's 30,000 telephones were cut off. The entire rail system was damaged. Most importantly, water mains were shattered. This meant that firemen did not have enough water to fight the fires. Fires burned for more than three days, destroying homes, busi-nesses, and government buildings. People gathered what belongings they could and headed to safe ground. Some 300,000 people were left homeless. Within a month, however, plans were underway to rebuild the city.

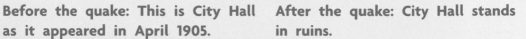

Before the quake: This is City Hall as it appeared in April 1905.

After the quake: City Hall stands in ruins.

After the quake, fires burned out of control throughout the city.

Building to Survive

If people choose to rebuild their towns and cities, they look for ways to make the area safer in case there are more earthquakes. Building on safer ground is one way. Another way is by making better and stronger buildings that will not collapse during an earthquake.

This building was not designed to survive an earthquake.

22

Scientists now have a way to test how well a building will stand up through an earthquake. First, they make a model of the building. Then they use a machine called an **earthquake table** to shake the model building just as a real earthquake would. If the model collapses when the earthquake table shakes, the scientists know the building was not built strongly enough. Using this information, scientists can teach new ways of making safer buildings. These new buildings will have a better chance of surviving another earthquake.

Researchers examine a scale model of an adobe house. The model was shaken to reproduce the effects of an earthquake and check the effects of a simple bracing system.

An earthquake shook up the city of San Francisco in 1989. But the city's tallest building wasn't even damaged. The building had been designed and built in a special way so that it could survive even a strong earthquake.

San Francisco's fifty-story TransAmerica Pyramid was built to withstand earthquakes.
- flexible upper stories
- pyramid shape resists shaking
- solid rock foundation moves with tremors

JAPANESE PAGODAS

The **pagodas** (puh-GO-duhz) of Japan look as though just a strong wind might blow them away. But they have survived hundreds of years— and many earth-quakes. The secret is in the way they are designed and built. They shake, but they don't fall down!

The East Pagoda of Taima-dera Temple in Nara, Japan, was built between 645 and 794 A.D.

25

On July 9, 1958, an 8.3 earthquake along the Fairweather Fault in Alaska triggered a debris avalanche. The avalanche created the largest known tsunami in history, which in turn stripped trees up to an elevation of 1,720 feet along Lituya Bay.

People may forget about earthquakes after a while. But earthquakes leave reminders by changing the way a whole area looks. Land that was hilly can become flat, and land that was flat can become hilly.

EARTHQUAKE LAKE

Reelfoot Lake

In the winter of 1811-1812, a series of earthquakes in Missouri changed the course of the mighty Mississippi River. The quakes were so strong that they made church bells ring in Boston, Massachusetts, a thousand miles away! That quake also turned a forest into a lake! If you look down into the lake today, you can still see treetops under the water. The lake is called Reelfoot Lake, but it is also known as Earthquake Lake. It is in the state of Kentucky.

Preparing for the Future

A seismologist studies cracks in the ground created by an earthquake.

Scientists who study earthquakes are called **seismologists**. They observe, study, and do experiments to learn more about what causes earthquakes and how to **predict** them. Their goal is to save lives, homes, towns, and cities. They work to make the world safer for everyone.

Go To ▶

Visit the U.S. Geological Survey earthquake website at **earthquake.usgs.gov** to learn more about earthquakes.

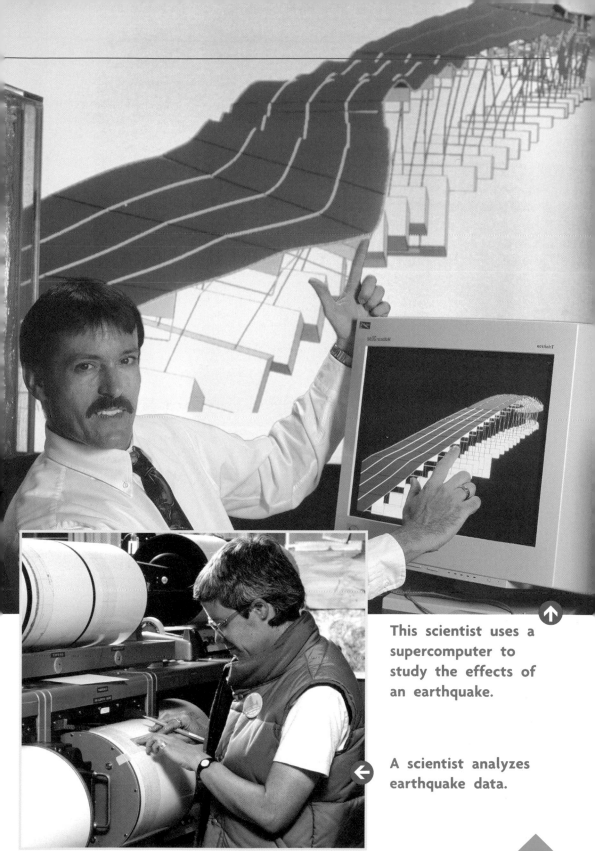

This scientist uses a supercomputer to study the effects of an earthquake.

A scientist analyzes earthquake data.

EARTHQUAKE SAFETY PRECAUTIONS

Earthquakes happen unexpectedly. Here are things you should know if you experience an earthquake. These tips were prepared by the Federal Emergency Management Agency.

1 If you are indoors during an earthquake, keep calm and take cover under a heavy table or desk. Stay away from glass, windows, or anything that could fall, like a bookcase.

2 If you are outdoors, move away from buildings, street lights, and utility wires.

3 If you are in a crowded public place, do NOT rush for the doors. Everyone will be doing that. Instead, take cover under something heavy and stay away from things that could fall on you. Stay calm. Do not get in an elevator during an earthquake!

4 After an earthquake, be prepared for aftershocks. They are dangerous because they can cause things that are weakened in the first earthquake to fall down.

5 If you are home and you smell gas or hear a hissing or blowing sound, open a window and get out of the building right away. It may mean that a gas line in your house has been broken. Tell your parent or another adult.

6 Make sure you are wearing shoes after an earthquake. There may be broken glass on the ground and inside your home.

Glossary

aftershock	shaking of the ground that comes after the main part of an earthquake
avalanches	ice and snow falling from the sides of mountains
earthquake	a shaking of the ground
earthquake table	a tool used to find out if buildings will stand or fall during an earthquake
landslides	dirt and rocks falling from the sides of mountains
pagodas	very old holy buildings in Japan
predict	say what will happen in the future
rubble	pieces of brick, concrete, and other materials left when a building falls down
seismogram	the record of an earth tremor
seismologist	a scientist who studies earthquakes
seismometer	a device that measures movements of the ground
tectonic plate	pieces of Earth's rocky crust that rub together or bump into each other, causing earthquakes
tsunami	a huge, dangerous wave that hits the shore after an earthquake; also called a tidal wave
vibration	shaking

Index